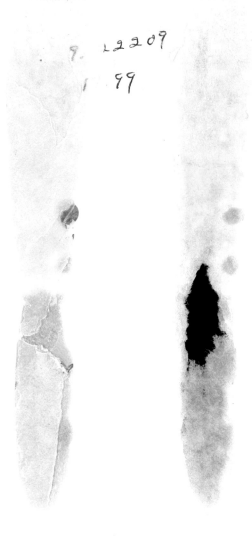

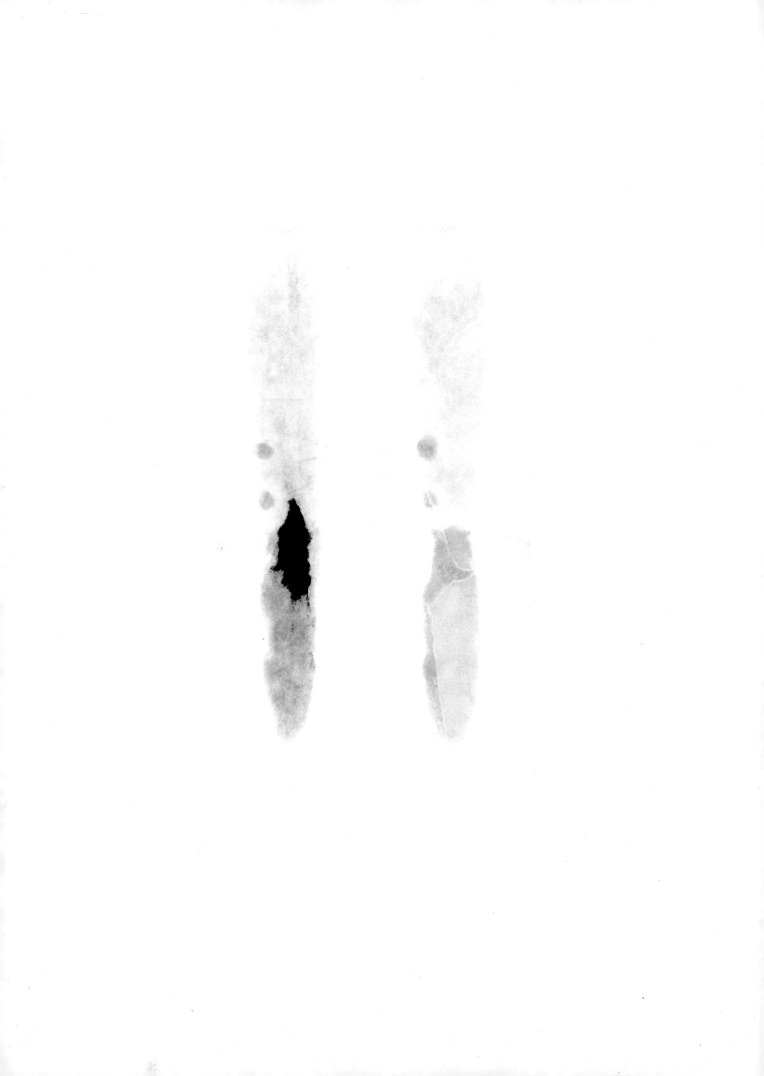

INVENTIONS
in science

The
CAR

STEVE PARKER

GLOUCESTER PRESS
NEW YORK • CHICAGO • LONDON • TORONTO • SYDNEY

*First published in the
United States in 1993 by*
Gloucester Press
95 Madison Avenue
New York, NY 10016

Printed in Belgium

Library of Congress
Cataloging-in-Publication Data

Parker, Steve.
    The car / Steve Parker.
        p.   cm. – (Inventions in
science)
    Includes index.
    Summary: Examines the
development of the modern car in all
its aspects and explores its social
impact.
    ISBN 0-531-17415-8
    1. Automobiles – History –
Juvenile literature. 2. Automobiles –
Social aspects – Juvenile literature. 3.
Automobiles – Design and construction
– Juvenile literature. [1. Automobiles –
History]
I. Title. II. Series.
TL147.P37 1993
629.222'09 – dc20
93-10812   CIP   AC

Design: David West
                Children's Book
                Design
Designer   Stephen
                Woosnam-Savage
Editor: Jen Green
Picture researcher: Emma Krikler
Illustrator: David Russell

Steve Parker is a writer and
editor in the life sciences,
health, and medicine, who has
written more than 50 books for
children on science and nature.

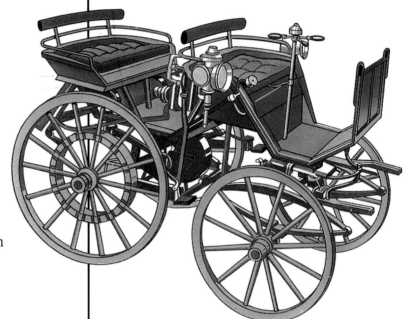

PHOTOCREDITS
Abbreviations: T-top, M-middle, B-bottom, L-left, R-right

*Front cover top and pages 6 left, 7, 8, 9 M & B, 10-11,
11 B, 22 L, & 30 ML: Mary Evans Picture Library;
front cover bottom and pages 18 R, 20 M, 22-23, 25 L
& R, 27 TR & 29 TL, R & M: Frank Spooner Pictures;
4 T & 24 L: Eye Ubiquitous; 4 BL, 5 B, 10 T, 19 B, 21
TL, M & B, 23 middle, 24-25, 30 T & 31 both: Roger
Vlitos; 4 BR: ELF; 5 T, 12, 14 B, 20 B, & 21 TR:
Charles de Vere; 6-7: Science Museum Library; 9 T & 14
T: Quadrant Photo Library; 13 L: Ford Cars; 15: Shell
Photo Services; 18 L & 19 T & M: Hulton Deutsch; 20
T, 27 TL & 29 BR: Spectrum Colour Library; 23 TL:
BMW Cars; 27 B: National Motor Museum at Beaulieu;
28 M: Renault UK.*

CONTENTS

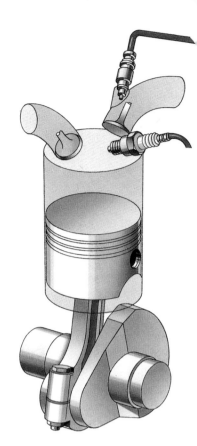

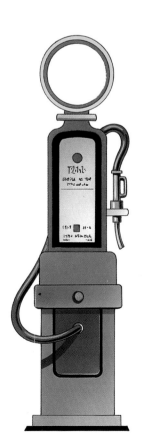

THE CAR TODAY

Since the first cars chugged along cart tracks almost 100 years ago, everyday life has changed beyond recognition. The car has played a major role in that transformation. Today we can jump into the car and drive to school, to work, or to a vacation halfway across the continent. Freeways and expressways crisscross the land. We can travel as far in one day as the old horse-drawn carriages traveled in a month. This is the story of the car: how it was invented, how it developed over the years, and how it has affected so many aspects of our lives and our world.

Too many cars?

Today traffic jams are a familiar sight in cities and on major roads all over the world. People waste time, and engines waste fuel. Many city centers are banning cars because of the noise, fumes, dirt, and traffic jams that cars cause. People are encouraged to use buses, trains, and bicycles, or to walk.

Police deal with traffic and cope with accidents

Pollution problems

Car exhaust fumes are a major cause of air pollution. They shower particles onto the surroundings and contain chemicals that react with sunlight to form choking smog. They also add to acid rain and global warming.

Eating up resources

Cars burn fuels made from petroleum (oil). They consume the world's limited supplies of petroleum at an amazing rate.

Car-making factories are major employers in many cities.

The car has transformed landscapes all over the world. Roads, parking lots, and roadside facilities take up more and more natural land. Gas stations must be sited at frequent intervals so that motorists do not run out of gas.

Leisure or shopping facilities will not attract customers unless people can drive and park there.

GO-KARTS

Work and play

In the modern world the car is used for both work and leisure activities. On a vacation by car we can drive when and where we wish and visit interesting places. Driving to and from work or school each day is often a less pleasurable experience. Noise, fumes, and traffic lines can make it stressful and sometimes dangerous. Yet many people say they "have to" use the car. They insist there is no alternative.

The modern car

The modern small car is a lightweight and efficient vehicle. It seats four or more people comfortably, and it is easy to handle in city centers or when cruising on the highway.

Service areas provide rest and food for travelers on long-distance journeys.

OUT

PIONEERS OF THE CAR

The motor car evolved from the horse-drawn carriage. The first cars, from the early 1800s, looked like horse-pulled carts with engines attached – indeed, they were called "horseless carriages." For inventors, the key was to develop an engine that was powerful and reliable enough to propel a wheeled vehicle along roads that were often muddy cart tracks. Some inventors tried to use the steam engine and some steam-powered vehicles were used in Britain in the 1830s. Others worked on a new source of power, the internal combustion engine, fueled by gasoline or diesel fuel.

Karl Benz
During the 1880s, German engineer Karl Benz worked on internal combustion engines powered by coal gas, and then by gasoline In 1885 he put one of these engines into a two-seater tricycle and created the first motorized cart, or motor car.

Cugnot's cannon-puller (above)
A French soldier, Nicholas-Joseph Cugnot, invented a three-wheeled steam tractor in about 1769. It was intended to replace horses for pulling army cannons. But when demonstrated before French generals, the tractor went out of control and the generals decided to keep their horses. In 1861 Canadian inventor Henry Seth Taylor attached a steam engine to a cart to form a steam carriage (above). Later steam was used to power cars, such as the Stanley Steamer. The steam engine was superseded by the internal combustion engine.

Daimler 1886

Gottlieb Daimler

Like Benz, Daimler was a German engineer. After working on gas-powered engines, he set up his own workshop in 1882. With engineer Wilhelm Maybach, he improved early gasoline-powered engines. In 1886, he built a four-wheeled vehicle powered by one of his 1.5-horsepower engines.

▲ Benz's Patent-Motorwagen dated from 1888

▼ **The Viktoria**

By 1887, Karl Benz was selling motorized tricycles to the rich and curious. At first they were merely spluttering toys. But people soon realized that these strange new vehicles could be big business. Benz's Viktoria, which appeared in 1890, was the first car to be made in appreciable numbers.

Motors and engines

The first practical internal combustion engine ran on gas and was invented by Belgian Etienne Lenoir in 1860. In 1876 German engineer Nicholas Otto improved it with the four-stroke cycle (see page 12). Daimler's early petrol engines ran at 900 rpm, much faster than the Otto engines. In the 1890s Rudolf Diesel invented the engine named after him (see page 13).

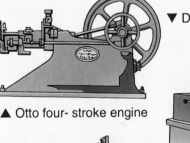

▲ Otto four- stroke engine

▼ Daimler gasoline engine

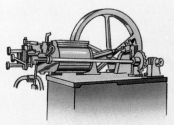

▼ Lenoir internal combustion gas engine

Diesel engine ▲

THE FIRST MOTORISTS

After the experiments of the 1880s, the first car-making factories were set up in Germany and France during the 1890s. Engineers improved Daimler's engines, making them more powerful and reliable. Frenchman Emile Levassor was probably first to think of the car as a machine in its own right, and not just a cart without a horse. In 1891 he moved the engine from the back to the front, away from the mud and stones thrown up by the wheels. He also replaced the belt drive between engine and road wheels, with a clutch and a gearbox. The car as we know it today was quickly taking shape.

Napier 1913

Fun for the family
A trip in the car was an enjoyable outing, provided the rain stayed away. Early cars had no heaters and little protection from mud, dust, or the weather.

Roads to run on
Cars were faster than horse-drawn carts, so they needed better roads. Instead of packed-down layers of earth and stone (top right), engineers devised smooth surfaces of tarmac or asphalt.

Drainage trench

Smooth asphalt surface

Graded gravel layers

Base of crushed stone

A sign of status
Big houses, fine furniture and beautiful horses had been signs of wealth for centuries. Around 1900 a new symbol of status appeared: the car. As yet, the car was not a useful means of transportation. Roads were muddy, rutted cart tracks, and refueling places were scarce.

Flying the red flag

Under a law passed in Britain in 1865, steam traction engines were allowed to lumber along roads, provided they did not exceed 4 mph (6.5 kph) and a man with a red flag walked about 170 feet in front. The red flag was abandoned in 1878, but a footman still had to walk 60 feet in front. This law applied to any similar vehicle, including the first cars. In 1896 the footman was abandoned too, and the speed limit raised to almost 12 mph (20 kph).

Gas pump 1905

Buying a car

At first, only the rich could afford a car. But many people gathered in car showrooms to gaze at these newfangled pieces of machinery, which seemed to have little practical use.

Stopping for fuel

In the early days many car owners carried cans of spare fuel with them. There were no detailed maps and finding a gasoline station on a long journey was mostly a matter of luck.

The maker's name

Car manufacturers were soon competing to produce the best, fastest, or cheapest vehicles. Companies such as Buick and Austin designed easily recognized nameplates.

Advertising

The growing car business involved designers, engineers, manufacturers, mechanics, and of course advertisers. As roads became busier, they became valuable places for posters, advertising the latest cars to drivers.

CARS FOR EVERYONE

During the early 1900s, most cars became larger, more comfortable – and more costly. In America, however, entrepreneur Henry Ford was working in the other direction. Ford understood that there were only a limited number of rich people. His aim was to build small cars in huge numbers, so that they were cheap enough for the average person to buy. This would allow families to travel by car where they wanted. It was part of the freedom offered by the "American Dream," in which Ford believed so strongly. And the dream came true, with the Model T Ford.

◀ Model T, 1914

Ford production line, 1913

The Model T

Production of the "Tin Lizzie" (so-called because the body was made of thin vanadium steel) began in 1908. The car had a four cylinder, three-liter, 20-horsepower engine, and a top speed of about 40 mph (65 kph). The Model T was designed to be inexpensive and long-lasting.

Production line

Ford claimed that "the way to make automobiles is to make one automobile like another automobile, to make them all alike." At first the Model Ts were made on Ford's new invention, the production line, in his Detroit factory. In 1913 he introduced the moving assembly line, which has since been copied around the world.

Mass motoring

When the Model T ceased production in 1927, more than 15 million had been made. Cheap motoring meant more crowded roads. Without clear road markings and signs, driving was a hazardous business.

"How many tunes does it play, mister?"

Cars in country areas were a source of bafflement. This postcard shows how the handcrank could be mistaken for the wind-up mechanism of a barrel organ!

Car versus Horse (1904)	
Total cost over five years A pair of horses, including food, stabling, vet's bills :	
	$4,780
Standard car, cost new:	$1,583
gas and oil:	$760
new set of tires:	$122
wages for boy to clean and maintain:	$633
repairs and spares:	$682
minus resale price:	$487
Total:	$3,293

The cost of cars

Ford set the cost trend with the Model T, and the more that were made, the cheaper they became. A basic version cost $825 when it was introduced, and $260 some years later.

Increasing choice

In the years before World War I, car manufacturers set up in most industrial countries. The home of mass production was America. European makers concentrated on the more expensive models built with hand tools, a development of the skilled tradition in building luxury horse-drawn carriages. Many famous names date from this period.

Peugeot 1905

Fiat 1914

Benz 1907

Mercedes 1914

ENGINES AND TRANSMISSION

The heart of any car is its engine. Over the years different types of engines have come and gone, including steam engines, gas power, and electric motors. But gasoline and diesel engines power almost all modern vehicles. They are called internal combustion engines because the power comes from the burning (combusting) of fuel inside the cylinder. A steam engine is an external combustion engine, because the fuel is burned outside the engine, to heat water in the boiler.

In the four-stroke cycle the piston moves up and down twice, giving four movements, or strokes, for each explosion of gasoline inside the cylinder.

▶ Modern twelve-cylinder five liter high performance BMW engine.

The gasoline engine
A modern gasoline engine is usually multi-cylindered. Inside each cylinder, a piston moves up and down as shown below. A system of cranks converts this up-and-down motion to the rotary motion of the crankshaft, which turns the gears in the gearbox, which turn the road wheels. Engine size or capacity is measured by the amount of air pushed out (displaced) from all the cylinders as the pistons move from their lowest to highest position. Today an average family car engine is about two liters.

1. Induction or intake stroke – descending piston sucks in mixture of air and fuel.

2. Compression stroke – rising piston squeezes mixture of air and fuel vapor.

3. Ignition or power stroke – spark plug ignites mixture, which explodes and pushes piston down.

4. Exhaust stroke – rising piston pushes out exhaust gases.

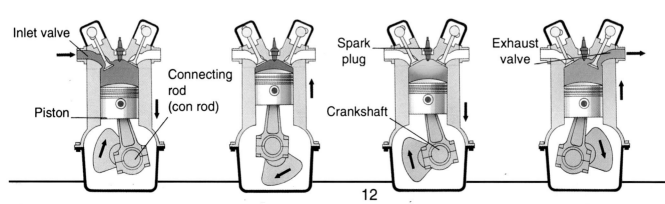

Inlet valve

Connecting rod (con rod)

Piston

Spark plug

Crankshaft

Exhaust valve

12

Transmission

This part of the car transmits the engine's power to the road wheels. A system of gears in the gearbox, driven by the crankshaft, allows the engine to turn at its most effective speed for different road speeds. In manual transmission, the driver shifts gear.

The clutch pedal works levers that disconnect the crankshaft from the gears, so that gears can be shifted and the car can stay still when the engine is turning. In automatic transmission, introduced in 1937, the gears are shifted automatically.

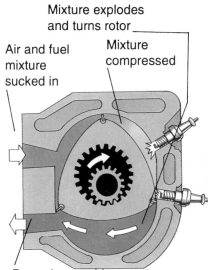

▲ Manual gear shift

▲ Automatic gearbox

Wankel engine

This engine was developed by German scientist Felix Wankel in 1956. It produces rotary movement directly. A three-sided, off-center rotor turns in a specially shaped chamber. The air and fuel mixture is sucked in, compressed and ignited, and blown out in a cycle similar to the normal engine. Several engines may be used to power one car. Problems with the Wankel engine include rapid engine wear, excessive fuel consumption, and weak engine seals.

Mixture explodes and turns rotor

Air and fuel mixture sucked in

Mixture compressed

Burned gases blown out

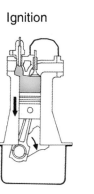

Induction   Compression

Ignition   Exhaust

Diesel engine

A diesel engine does not have spark plugs. The air-fuel mixture is at high pressure, and becomes so hot that it ignites itself. Diesel engines last longer than gasoline engines and are becoming lighter and quieter.

Peugeot front-wheel drive car

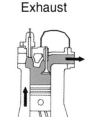

Drive layouts

Since about 1900, most cars have had the engine at the front. Driving the two rear road wheels by a long propeller (transmission) shaft gives good weight distribution, stability and traction. Front wheel drive gives increased traction, but may alter the weight distribution. Four-wheel drive gives excellent traction.

Four-wheel drive

Front-wheel drive

Rear-wheel drive

13

FUEL AND IGNITION

A car engine does not work unless its fuel is delivered in exactly the right amounts, at the right times, mixed with the right volume of air, so that it will burn. This is the job of the fuel and ignition systems. Several methods for mixing the air and fuel were developed, leading to the creation of the carburetor that could adjust the amounts of fuel and air according to the engine's speed and the load on it. As for ignition, the original Daimler engines had a platinum pipe in the top of the cylinder, which glowed red hot when heated by a burner at the other end, and ignited the fuel. Today electronic ignition systems and spark plugs do the job.

Carburetors

Fuel will not burn without oxygen from the air. The carburetor draws fuel from the fuel tank and makes it into a very fine spray, which mixes with the correct amount of air.

Early carburetor, 1919 ▶

Spark plugs

In a fast-running engine, each spark plug fires many times every second, to set fire to the fuel-air mixture inside the cylinder. The spark leaps across a gap at the tip of the plug, between the central electrode and the outer angled electrode. Up to 30,000 volts are needed to make each spark – far more than the usual 12-volt car battery can supply. The voltage is increased by a device called an ignition coil, using the principle of electrical induction.

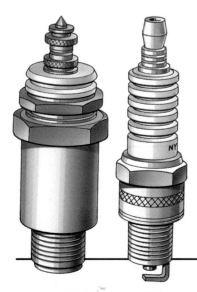

Distributor (left)

This feeds (distributes) high-voltage electricity to each spark plug at precisely the right moment, just as the piston below is compressing the fuel-air mixture. In many cars the distribution system is now electronic, controlled by a microchip.

Fuel injector

Spark plug

Inlet valve opens

Piston

Crankshaft

Fuel injection

As early as 1902, French engineer Amédée Bollée devised a system of fuel injection. Normally the air flowing into the piston sucks the fuel in with it. The fuel injector forces in extra amounts of fuel, using the pressure created by an electric motor-pump. This gives a better fuel-air mixture, and so a more powerful combustion stroke. Fuel injection involves more working parts and more fine-tuning than an ordinary system. Turbochargers are usually fitted only to high-performance cars.

Turbo power

A turbocharger has a fan-shaped turbine blade that is turned by the exhaust gases (below). It compresses air so a better fuel-air mixture can be forced into the cylinder.

To the engine

Pressurized air

Air

Exhaust gases

Computer car

Since 1966, when electronic fuel injection was developed, microchips have become more common in cars. They sense the load on the engine, monitor the air and fuel flow to the engine, and adjust the carburetor and fuel injection to give the best performance.

More recently, electronics can tell the driver about faults in the oil or hydraulic systems, brakes, tires, and even burned-out bulbs, as well as helping with route planning (above right).

A silicon chip

The fuel industry

Car fuels are made from petroleum oil. So are jet fuels, engine lubricating oils, solvents, plastics, detergents, paints, tars, asphalts, and hundreds of other products. These substances are separated and purified from the dark, thick crude petroleum at giant oil refineries. The vast quantities of fuels used by cars, trucks, and other vehicles mean that the car and oil industries often work together to develop more efficient and cleaner fuels.

CHASSIS, BRAKES, AND TIRES

The first cars had a framework or chassis built of wood and metal, as horse-pulled carriages did. As cars became faster and more powerful, the chassis had to be stronger in order to cope with the stresses. But fast driving over rutted roads was very uncomfortable. Suspension systems were invented, so that the road wheels could bounce over holes and bumps while the main body of the car stayed level. Air-filled tires made the ride smoother, and better brakes made it safer.

White, 1905

The old chassis
The chassis was the car's "skeleton," usually made of metal girders. All the main parts, such as the engine, seats, axles, and bodywork, were bolted or fixed to it.

Suspension
Prior to the 1960s most cars had both wheels on one axle at the rear, and independent suspension at the front. Now cars often have independent suspension all around, so each wheel can move up or down on its own. Telescopic shock absorbers (below) reduce the tendency of springs to bounce up and down.

Active suspension
In computer-controlled active suspension, sensors detect the movements of the road wheels and feed information to pumps that control the amounts of oil in the suspension unit cylinders. Large jolts can be smoothed out by quickly pumping extra oil into or out of the cylinders. The suspension can also be "stiffened" when cornering fast, to stop the car from tilting too much.

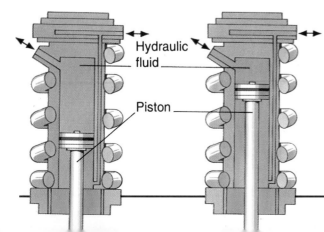

Hydraulic fluid

Piston

As the car hits a bump, fluid is pushed out as piston moves up, to dampen the bouncing of the spring.

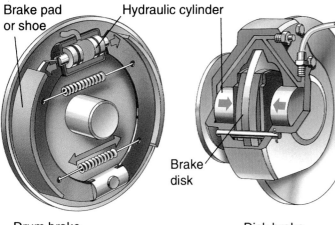

Brake pad or shoe   Hydraulic cylinder

Brake disk

Drum brake   **Disk brake**

Brakes

The first cars had bicycle-type brake-blocks. Greater speeds needed more effective brakes. In 1902 Louis Renault made brake shoes which pressed on the inside of a revolving drum fixed to the wheel – the drum brake. In the disk brake, designed later by Frederick Lanchester, pads press on a revolving metal disk.

Wheels

Like horse-drawn carriages, early cars had large wheels, some more than one yard across, because the roads of the time had such deep holes! Soon wooden spokes were replaced by solid metal disks, made lighter by a pattern of holes. Modern low-profile wheels are lighter still, allowing for wider tires.

Spoked wheel   Pressed-steel wheel   Low-profile wheel

Tires

Pneumatic (air-filled) tires, developed from the bicycle tires pioneered by John Dunlop in 1888, were quickly adapted for use on cars. A modern tire is made up of many layers.

Water-shedding tread pattern

Rubber covering

Rayon layer

Steel reinforcing belts

Nylon lining

Wire-reinforced rim

One-piece car
Studebaker of America began to build steel chassis and all-steel bodies in the early 1920s. But few modern cars have a separate chassis. The usual design is the "monocoque" or unitary construction, pioneered by Citroën in 1934. Compartments for the engine, passengers, and luggage are all part of the same steel structure.

Monocoque chassis

THE GOLDEN ERA

The two World Wars of 1914-18 and 1939-45 stimulated progress in many areas of science and engineering – including the car. After World War II, shortages of steel and gasoline meant a delay before the new models appeared. When they arrived, they were much more powerful and sleeker than their predecessors. As the shortages faded, a new generation of well-off teenagers was growing up in the major industrial countries. For them, cars were symbols of youth, style, and freedom.

The gas-guzzlers
During the 1950s, especially in America, cars became subjects of strange fashions. Cadillacs, Chevrolets, and Studebakers appeared in gaudy colors, and sprouted tail fins, grilles, and yards of shiny chrome plate. Their huge engines consumed large amounts of "gas" (gasoline or petrol), but the newly rich youngsters could easily afford it – at least, their parents could.

The teen dream
Young people of the 1950s and 60s rapidly adopted fast cars and motorcycles for their own generation. The difference between these powerful new machines and the old, slow cars reflected the generation gap between them and their parents.

Ford Thunderbird (T-bird) Coupé, 1956 ▶

"Ridin' along in my automobile"
Cars were a favorite subject of many pop songs by Chuck Berry (right), the Beach Boys, and others. Young people shook off the war memories and took to a new, relaxed life-style as they cruised along highways.

The 1960s

The 1960s was the age of the small car. The German "Beetle" became immensely popular, and the British Mini's revolutionary design was partly a reaction to the huge cars of the 1950s. With front-wheel drive, and all-around rubber suspension, the Mini was fun to drive and easy to park. It was an instant success, and became a symbol of the fashionable "Swinging London."

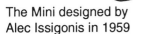

Volkswagen Beetle launched in 1935

The Mini designed by Alec Issigonis in 1959

Cars in daily life

By the 1960s, cars were no longer merely a means of transportation. They were an essential part of many events in daily life. New towns were designed with car-owners in mind. Drive-in cinemas, restaurants, banks, and even drive-in churches flourished. Parking lots took over great areas of land, so that workers could park near their factories and shoppers near their stores. The car was also a place where courting couples could be alone, and each town had its secluded "Lover's Lane."

A place to park

The 1960s trend toward high-rise buildings affected cars, too. New methods of mixing and pouring concrete made possible the construction of multi-level garages. These were one solution to parking in city centers.

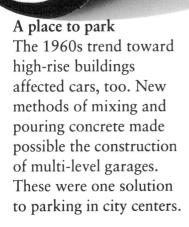

IN-CAR ENTERTAINMENT

In the early years of cars, roads were small and narrow. They wound through towns and villages. Travelers enjoyed the countryside, stopped for rests and to visit places of interest, and broke long journeys by overnight stays. In the 1950s and 60s, freeways and expressways were built across the landscape, wide and straight. Drivers could cover hundreds of miles in a day. Along with the faster cars being developed, these roads opened up new possibilities for reaching faraway destinations on car trips. But there was a new problem: how to fill all those in-car hours.

Style and comfort

A limousine is a large luxury car. It has deep, padded, reclining seats, and "extras" such as air conditioning. The stretch-limo has an extra section in the middle, making it even longer, so that passengers have plenty of leg room. These expensive cars are ideal for long journeys. They are quiet and comfortable, and often equipped with TV, phone, and even a cocktail bar.

A stretch-limo ▶

Motown

In the 1920s many car makers set up in Detroit: Ford, General Motors, Packard, Hudson, Maxwell, and Dodge. In the 1960s a soul-based rhythmic music from Detroit became known as Motown, after the city's nickname, Motor Town. Diana Ross (left) was one of Motown's most famous stars

Car phones

As the roads swell with more and more cars, so journey times are increasing, particularly in crowded areas. Mobile car phones allow motorists to be in contact with the office, family, and friends. The range of car phones can vary according to the type of system used, from local to international.

In-car music

In 1922 the "father of radio" Guglielmo Marconi experimented with the British Daimler Company on car radios. Today's hi-fi multi-speaker car radio systems have come a long way since then. Other types of car music machines appeared as early as the 1900s. First came waxed cylinders, which rotated as a stylus (needle) played in the wavy groove in the wax. Next came vinyl record-players (phonograms), and cassettes. Modern cars are often fitted with Compact Disc (CD) players that use laser beams to read the microscopic humps and pits on the disc that encode the sounds.

Cassette player from the 1960s

Modern programmable CD player

At your fingertips

As early as 1929, car radios were being offered as extras by several American manufacturers. A modern family car bristles with gadgets (below). Most are within easy reach of the driver and operate by simple controls, so that he or she is not distracted. The radio, cassette tape, CD player, and computer are common fittings.

Traffic information

Many radio stations (above) broadcast traffic news to give drivers advance warning of construction, accidents, and traffic tie-ups. These stations may gather their information from the police, spotter planes and helicopters, the patrols of road organizations, and drivers who phone in with up-to-the-minute details.

COMFORT AND SAFETY

Sitting in the warmth of the latest family saloon, it is difficult for us to appreciate that the first cars were very drafty and uncomfortable, with leaky canvas roofs and no heating. Improvements have come gradually over the years, beginning with the first enclosed car in 1895, by makers Panhard. The windshield was offered as an "optional extra" in 1899, by manufacturers Dietrich-Bollée, and windshield wipers were first used by Cadillac in 1915. In recent years, safety in high-speed crashes has become an extremely important factor to consider when buying a car.

Keeping warm

At one time, motorists would not dream of setting off without a warm coat and hat, gloves, and a travel rug for body and legs. An open car traveling at high speed could be a cold place, even on the sunniest days. The first car heaters took warmth from the engine exhaust, and were introduced in the United States in 1905. In 1926 heaters began to use warmth from the hot water in the engine's cooling system. Power-operated windows appeared in 1946, again in the U.S.

▶ In some modern cars, an air bag inflates to protect the driver in a crash.

Air conditioning

The car air conditioning system cools air or warms it, humidifies (adds moisture) or dries it, and removes dust and smells, so that passengers remain comfortable. Air conditioning is useful in hot climates, especially when cars become stuck in long traffic jams. The benefit is not solely increased comfort. A motorist who becomes too hot and sticky may begin to drive less carefully.

▼ Refrigerated air from a separate cooling system is mixed with air from the normal heating system in controlled amounts.

Thermostat

Radiator

Air flow control

Air outlets

Testing

Every new type of car has to pass a long list of safety tests. Some involve crashing the car at high speed, to test the strength of the passenger section. Bumpers (fenders), brakes, lights, steering, fuel system, and traction are also checked, on the prototypes and then on selected samples from the production lines, before the car receives a certificate of roadworthiness.

Belting up

Seat belts first appeared in the 1920s. The modern seat belt adjusts and allows its wearer to move about in normal traveling. But if the car suddenly jerks, the belt locks to prevent the wearer from being hurled forward. Many countries now have laws enforcing the wearing of seat belts.

Computer design

Nowadays, manufacturers depend heavily on computers. In CAD (Computer Aided Design), computer programs work out the streamlining of a particular design, how this affects fuel use, how much metal it would take to make the car body, and its strength in a crash.

The safety cage

Today's cars usually have a stiffened "cage" around the passengers, with strengthening metal girders. Engine and luggage compartments form "crumple zones" that absorb the shock of a front or rear crash.

ECONOMY AND POLLUTION

Almost since Daimler and Benz put their pioneering vehicles on the market, there have been big, expensive cars and small, cheap ones. Most drivers bought the best they could afford. But the 1970s and 80s brought a new awareness. People began to understand about pollution and the need to preserve the countryside, and about conserving natural resources such as petroleum. The "green movement" spread, and the car was one of its main targets. Many people turned to smaller cars, which used less fuel and caused less pollution.

Cleaning up the car

In 1940, there were about 50 million cars in the world. Today, there are more than 400 million, and the number is rising steadily. The noise, dust, smog, and smells caused by cars are a problem, especially in cities. In addition, car exhausts contain the gases carbon monoxide and carbon dioxide, which contribute to the environmental problem of global warming, and nitrous oxides, which cause acid rain. People have begun to demonstrate about the damage that millions of cars are doing to the environment. Some protests are even staged on bicycles (below). Car makers have responded by building smaller, more economical vehicles. Their ads emphasize engine efficiency, safety, less pollution, and streamlining, which looks good and increases fuel economy. Some new cars are designed so that metals and other materials can be recycled.

Lead-free gasoline

Since 1923, a chemical called ethyl lead has been added to gasoline. This makes the engine run more smoothly, without "knocking" (see page 31). However, scientific research has shown that lead is dangerous to the body, even in tiny quantities. It can cause brain damage. People who breathe the dense lead fumes from car exhausts around busy roads may be at risk of mental and learning problems. So most countries now encourage motorists to buy cars that run on unleaded gasoline.

CATALYTIC CONVERTERS

A catalytic converter is fitted to a vehicle with an internal combustion engine. It is a special chamber in the exhaust pipe which filters out hazardous fumes from the engine, carrying out three chemical reactions to get rid of three main pollutants. A good catalytic converter cuts down emissions of nitrous oxides, the gases that help to make acid rain, by nine-tenths. Since 1981, catalytic converters have been required by law on new cars produced in the U.S. European countries are also introducing laws concerning catalytic converters.

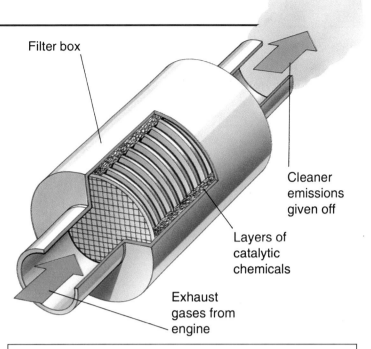

Filter box

Cleaner emissions given off

Layers of catalytic chemicals

Exhaust gases from engine

▼ A tiny Japanese "compact"

Major manufacturers
In 1950, the U.S. made two-thirds of the world's motor vehicles. By 1980 this share had gone down to about one-fifth. Japan had overtaken Britain, then Germany, and finally the U.S., to become the world's main vehicle-making country. This is partly due to the working methods in Japanese factories, and also to investment in automatic "robot" welders, assemblers, and painters.

MOTOR VEHICLE PRODUCTION
in thousands of vehicles

	U.S.	Britain	France	Germany	Japan
1930	2363	237	230	71	0.5
1950	8006	784	358	306	32
1970	8284	2098	2750	3842	5289
1980	8010	1313	3378	3878	11049
1990	9780	1566	3769	5148	13487

THE ELECTRIC CAR

The electric car seems to solve many of today's car-caused problems. In an internal combustion engine, less than half the energy in the fuel is converted into useful energy, to power the car. In an electric motor, this figure is nine-tenths. Electric cars are quiet, efficient, and give off no poisonous fumes. So why don't we all use them? There are various reasons, particularly the limitations of the batteries, which need to be recharged frequently. People who are used to the convenience of a gasoline or diesel engine would find an electric car restricting for this reason.

A century of electric cars

The electric car is not a new idea. Powerful electric motors and batteries were developed late in the last century.

By 1900, several electric cars were available to the public. Henry Ford considered electric motors and also gas engines for his cars, before deciding on internal combustion.

Modern prototype electric car

The Hybrid

This is both electric and gasoline-driven – a hybrid. Its batteries can usually be kept fully charged from the mains. On long journeys, a small engine drives a generator that makes enough electricity to keep the batteries charged. Individual electric motors drive each road wheel. Since the shafts of the motors turn powerfully at low speeds, this type of car needs no gears.

▼ The Hybrid power car

Batteries

Generator

Electric motor

Better batteries

Normally batteries in an electric car restrict journeys to about 120 miles. If the batteries have to be recharged, the vehicle is out of action. Battery technology is advancing, with the development of rechargeable NiCad (Nickel-Cadmium), Lithium, and other fuel cells (right), but progress is steady rather than spectacular. A breakthrough in the next few years looks unlikely. One solution would be to make battery-changing centers as common as gasoline stations.

Electric motor

Electric vehicles

Electrically-powered vehicles are a familiar sight as golf carts and small carts used in large shopping centers. These vehicles travel relatively short distances, and their electric motors cope efficiently with constant stopping and starting. The drivers can return to base and pick up a freshly-charged vehicle when necessary.

The electric trike

The Sinclair C5 was launched in 1985. It had a small electric motor and was assisted by pedal-power from the driver. But it was slow and vulnerable in traffic.

Other energy sources

Today's cars could be improved by using the internal combustion engine more efficiently. As a car brakes, energy is lost as heat in the brake drums or disks. One idea is to transfer the energy of the slowing car to a heavy flywheel, making it spin faster as the car slows. This energy could then be "recycled" back to the road wheels as the car accelerates again (below). Another idea is to use renewable fuels, obtained from plants such as oilseed-rape or sugar cane.

▲ Sinclair C5

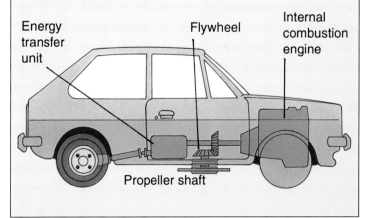

Energy transfer unit

Flywheel

Internal combustion engine

Propeller shaft

THE FUTURE

Karl Benz and Gottlieb Daimler would be amazed, and perhaps horrified, to see the way their inventions have affected the world. What lies in the future? Cars give us so much personal freedom, to go where and when we wish, that people are unlikely to choose to give them up. Unless public transportation improves massively, it cannot offer an alternative, especially for those in rural areas. One way forward may be to make cars simpler and more efficient, so that we can enjoy our freedom, while needing to worry less about polluting and destroying our world.

More cars

Car use is rocketing. About 70 new cars drive onto the world's roads *every minute*. In the United States, the number of cars more than doubled between 1960 and 1990. No sooner is a large new roadway completed, than it is filled bumper-to-bumper. Governments agree that cars create pollution problems, and consume natural resources. But moves to restrict car use would be unpopular. A government that introduced such measures would be unlikely to be reelected.

Third World demand

As Third World countries develop, car use rises dramatically. If there were as many cars in Third World countries as there are in the West, the effect on the environment would be catastrophic. But developing countries have as much right to cars as western countries.

The future – now?

Tomorrow's cars will probably be made from lightweight, corrosion-proof materials, such as special plastics and metal alloys. They will be even sleeker, to cut down wind resistance and to increase fuel economy. Cars like the electric Renault Zoom (left) may contract to make parking easy.

▲ The car of the future?

Predicting the future

In years gone by, experts predicted all kinds of amazing advances in the car. One common idea was that cars would lose their road wheels and be able to counteract gravity, and so "float" above the ground like mini-hovercraft. Some predictions, such as greater streamlining and more use of plastics, have come true. However, the basic gasoline engine, steering wheel, gears, and four road wheels still remain.

▶ 1960s prediction

▼ 1980s prediction

▼ 1990s electric car

Action against pollution

Traffic fumes and smog are so bad in some cities that they are a public health hazard. Los Angeles has identified electric vehicles as one way to reduce the problem. The city intends to have one-tenth of vehicles running on electricity by 2000.

Making cars

Car factories are becoming more automated. Computers and robots carry out the tedious jobs of assembling cars, piece by piece, accurately and tirelessly (see below). But there will probably always be a small demand for special cars, hand-made to meet customers' requirements.

Fuels of the future

If we continue to burn gasoline, diesel, and other petroleum-based fuels at today's rates, the petroleum still in the ground will run out in 50-100 years. Can we improve engine efficiency? Yes. Most cars travel about 18-20 miles per gallon of fuel. Test cars being developed now can run over 60 miles per gallon. Another possibility is solar power – using the energy in sunlight to make electricity for electric cars. In 1987 the experimental car Sunraycer crossed Australia using solar power generated by solar panels, as in the prototype pictured below.

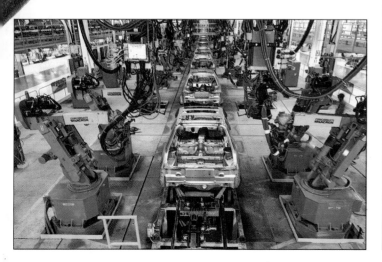

CHRONOLOGY

1885 Karl Benz makes his three-wheeled engine-driven carriage, the first practical car

1886 Gottlieb Daimler builds a four-wheeled car with a gasoline engine

1891 Daimler's Mercedes model becomes the first true "car" as we would recognize it today

1891 Levassor and Panhard begin building front-engined cars

1893 First U.S. gasoline-powered automobile, built by the Duryea brothers

1895 André and Edouard, the Michelin brothers, devise pneumatic tires

1897 The Stanley Steamer becomes famous

1899 Daimler invents the water-filled cooling radiator

1902 First volume production car–the Oldsmobile

1903 The first "speed traps" are organized in the U.S.

1904 Automatic transmission fitted by Sturtevant in the U.S.; Michelin bring in tire tread patterns for better grip in the wet

1905 The first car theft occurs, in St. Louis, Missouri

1906 Charles Rolls and Henry Royce introduce the Silver Ghost

1908 Henry Ford makes the first Model Ts

1910 A public drive-in "gas station" opens in

▼ Oldsmobile 1904

Detroit, Michigan

1912 First cars fitted with electric starters, making cars "more popular with the ladies"

1913 Ford introduces the moving assembly line

1913 The first direction indicators (swinging arms)

1914 The first stop sign is erected – in Detroit

1915 The first windshield wipers offered on Cadillacs

▲ Austin Tourer

1919 Three-color traffic lights are introduced – in Detroit

1919 Servo-assisted brakes are devised by Hispano-Suiza

1921 Hydraulic (pressure-oil) systems fitted to the Duesenberg Model A

1922 Austin launches the Seven, a tiny 4-seater with a 747cc (0.747 liter) engine

1923 Pratts (later Esso) put lead additives in petrol

1927 Chrome plating on Oldsmobiles and Studebakers

1929 The first synchromesh gearbox is fitted to a production car, by Cadillac

1931 Swallow Coachbuilding show their SS1, later to become the Jaguar

1933 The first drive-in cinema opens in New Jersey

1934 The new Citroën has a monocoque chassis construction, independent suspension and front-wheel drive

1935 Parking meters appear in Oklahoma City, Olklahoma

1937 Windshield washers are fitted to some Studebakers

1938 Germany launches the KDF, or Volkswagen "Beetle"

1940 Automatic transmission offered as standard on Chrysler-Oldsmobiles

1944 U.S. establishes its interstate highway system

1945 Dippable headlights begin with Philips' two-

▼ 1942 Cadillac coupé

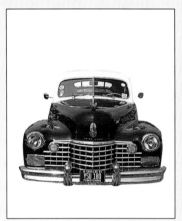

filament bulb

1947 Tubeless tires introduced by Goodrich

1947 A new Italian manufacturer, Ferrari, announces a 1.5-liter 12-cylinder sports car

1948 Radial tires brought in by Michelin

1948 Jaguar's XK120 is capable of 120 mph

1949 The first large tail-fins appear on Cadillacs

1950 Dunlop patents a new type of disk brake

GLOSSARY

▲ Toyota Space Cruiser

1951 Power steering becomes standard on many quality cars
1954 Tubeless tires are now standard
1956 Wankel engine is demonstrated
1957 Fuel injection is fitted to ordinary

▲ BMW Isetta

production cars
1959 BMC launch the revolutionary Mini
1961 The Renault R4's cooling system is sealed for life
1963 Wankel rotary engine is fitted to the rear-engined German NSU Spider
1966 Electronic fuel systems developed in

Britain
1968 U.S. introduced first laws to control car exhaust pollutants
1969 Experiments are made with an air bag that inflates to protect the driver in a crash
1971 Engines are modified to use unleaded gasoline
1974 New cars in America have catalytic converters
1977 Experiments with hydrogen gas as a fuel
1980 The Audi Quattro has four-wheel drive
1984 Mercedes-Benz brings in ABS (Anti-Lock Braking System)
1986 BMW develop in-car computerized systems
1987 Sunraycer solar-powered car crosses Australia using rechargeable silver-zinc batteries
1990 Electric cars are launched by Peugeot and Fiat

Active suspension
A computer-controlled system that keeps the car body at a fixed height above the ground by adjusting the suspension at each wheel.

Air bag
A safety device mounted on the steering wheel. The bag inflates in the event of a collision, to prevent chest injuries to the driver.

Anti-lock braking system (ABS)
A computer-controlled braking system. ABS applies and releases brake pressure to individual wheels to prevent wheel lock and skidding in poor weather conditions.

Capacity
Engine size, measured by the amount of air displaced by its cylinders during one cycle.

Catalytic converter
A special filter fitted to modern exhaust systems. It contains chemicals which remove pollutants from exhaust gases.

Chassis
The framework of a car, to which the engine, wheels and body are attached.

Computer Aided Design (CAD)
A computerized system which aids the design of modern cars.

Computer management
A computer system now

fitted to many high-performance cars. It monitors the engine and makes adjustments to maintain fuel efficiency.

Crankshaft
The rod or shaft which concerts the up and down (oscillating) movement of the pistons into a rotary (turning) movement to drive the wheels.

Fuel injection
A means of supplying the engine cylinders with extra fuel in accurate, controlled doses.

Knocking
Also known as pinking or detoning, is caused by faulty tuning of the engine. It occurs when the air-fuel mixture in the cylinders is igniting too early or too quickly, which makes a metallic "knock" or "pink."

Monocoque
One-piece car chassis, pioneered by Citroën in 1934.

Safety cage
A reinforced structure around the passenger compartment to reduce injury in a collision.

Transmission
The system of gears and shafts which transmits the turning of the engine to the wheels.

Turbocharger
A pump driven by the engine's exhaust, which improves the fuel-air mixture fed to the cylinders, and so gives better engine performance.

INDEX